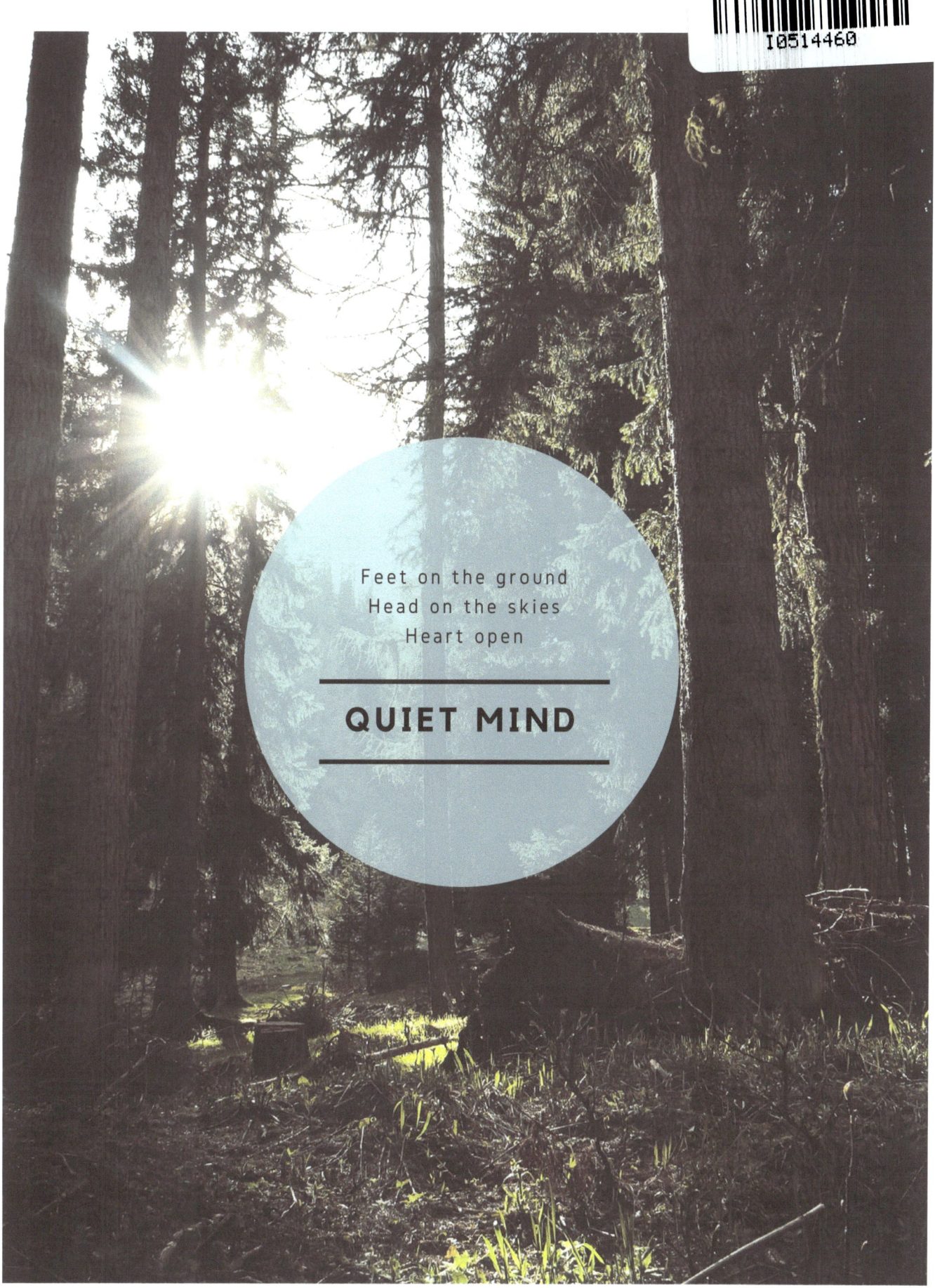

I am indebted to the following people who have been more than generous with their support, advice, encouragement, expertise, and experience:

Michael McGee
Maire Ní Chasaide
Josie Doohan
Paddy McHugh
Solas team
All the participants from Solas group.

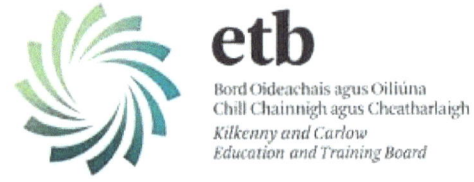
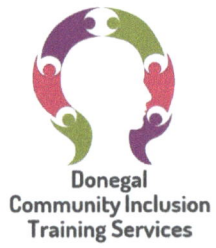
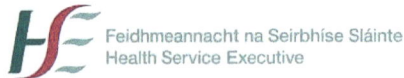

SOLAS

Solas Donegal is an outdoor walking programme that supports mental health recovery.

Our programme is based on an Ecotherapy model which utilises the healing properties of the natural environment to improve our health. This is also known as Green Exercise and has proven benefits specifically for our mental health. Walking is recognised as an excellent form of exercise and connection to others is vital for our mental wellbeing.

Being outdoors in nature, away from technology and the stresses of modern day life can significantly boost our mood and improve our physical health. Exercising in nature has also been shown to improve our concentration and creative thinking.

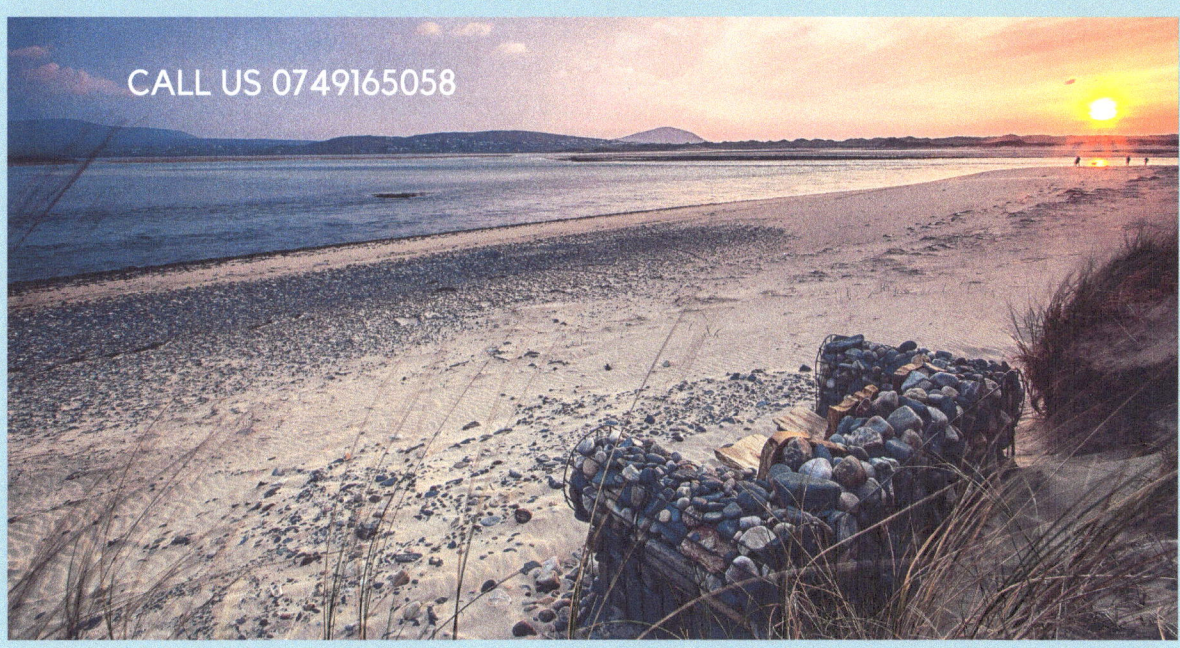

CALL US 0749165058

Exercise promotes better sleep patterns and can lower blood pressure. Walking side by side with other people helps us connect and makes it easier to talk. Research also shows that this helps improve our self esteem and our ability to cope with life stressors. All of this boosts our resilience. The basis of Solas Donegal is walking, talking and listening in nature.

Solas Donegal aims to support each person's recovery journey, building confidence, developing positive relationships and instilling hope for the future. The opportunity to share experiences and enjoy the interaction with other group members is a central part of the programme.

We use a number of therapeutic supports, including group discussion, reflection, goal setting and mindfulness. The practice of mindfulness brings awareness to the present moment and teaches us to be more compassionate towards ourselves and others.

We currently have two locations in Donegal, the scenic coastal towns of Falcarragh and Buncrana. Donegal is fortunate to have some of the most beautiful green spaces in Ireland with our hills, beaches, forests, and islands! Solas Donegal takes full advantage of this and our walks are different every day.

Solas Donegal is a HSE programme which has been running since 2005.

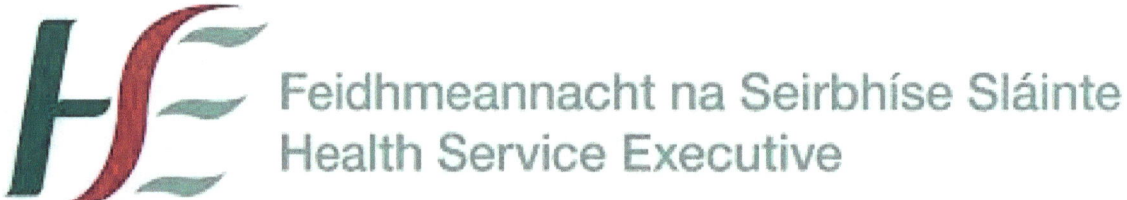

CALL US 0749165058

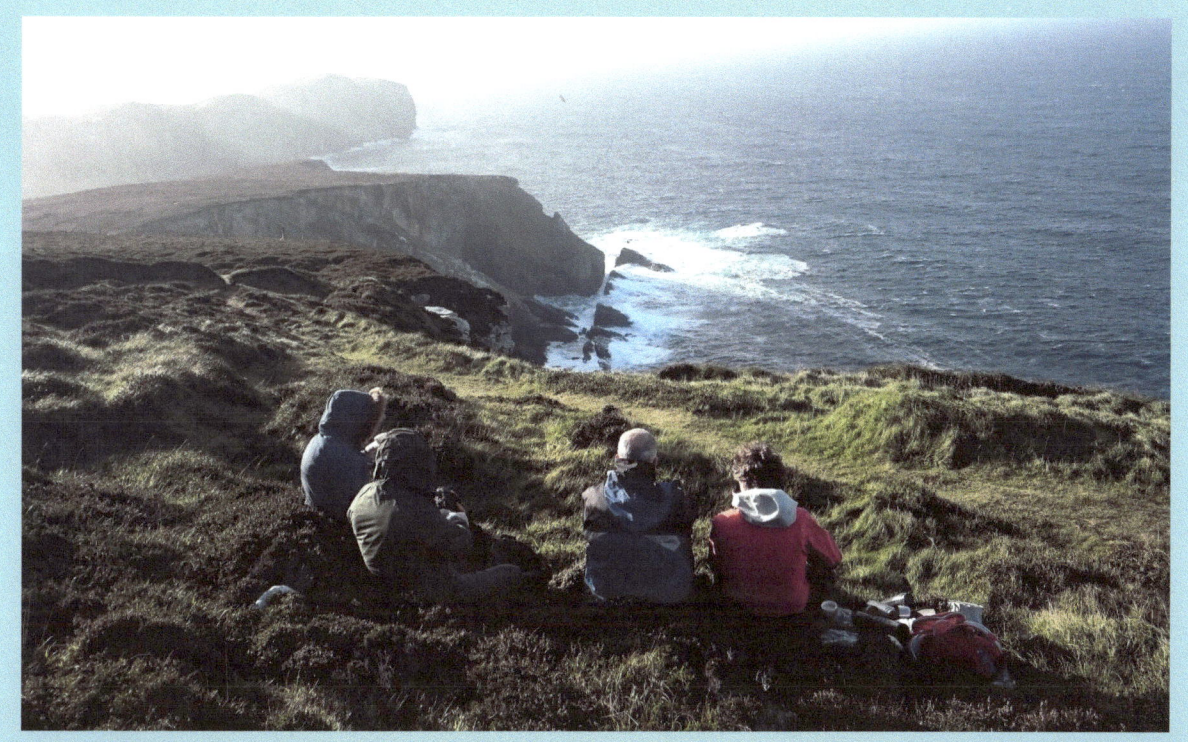

"A FEW SIMPLE TIPS FOR LIFE: FEET ON THE GROUND, HEAD TO THE SKIES, HEART OPEN…QUIET MIND." — RASHEED OGUNLARU

To complete the cycle relating to the outdoor activity, the particpants will gather material from the outdoors, will contemplate and feel it, then transform it into something real and tangible.

ANTSEANBHEAIRIC

This authentic two-storey building was originally constructed in 1890 as the Falcarragh Police Barracks and used as such until 1920 when it became the Falcarragh Garda Station. This period in history coincides with the most memorable time in the development of the Irish Republic and therefore the building has witnessed some dramatic events. Permanent exhibits of the history and culture of the Barracks are displayed within the visitor centre, which adds to the uniqueness and authenticity of the centre.

Tógadh an foirgneamh dhá urlár seo i dtús báire sa bhliain 1890 mar Bheairic Péas an Fháil Charraigh. Mhair sé mar sin go dtí gur haistríodh anonn chuig na Gardaí Síochána é sa bhliain 1920. Sa lá atá inniu tá An tSean Bheairic ina chuisle Ghealach ar bhaile an Fhál Carraigh, le caifé bríomhar, siopa céardaíochta, ionad oidhreachta agus turasóireachta, chomh maith le amharclann agus seomraí ilfheidhmeach.

Heritage Centre
The Heritage Centre includes exhibits which tell the history of the area. An tSean Bheairic has produced two audio-visual displays which are available to view in the centre which reveal the history of the area and the history of policing in the area. The Fáilte Ireland Visitor Information Point provides information on accommodation, places to eat, routes to take, maps, guides and books, places to visit, things to do and details on national and local events. Gifts, souvenirs, local craft, books and CD's are available in the Craft Shop. The Coffee Shop serves a range of sandwiches, panini's and wraps along with a selection of cakes. The Centre hosts events ranging from music concerts and festivals to book launches and art exhibitions.

> "EVERY EXPERIENCE, NO MATTER HOW BAD IT SEEMS, HOLDS WITHIN IT A BLESSING OF SOME KIND. THE GOAL IS TO FIND IT." — BUDDHA

The art-craft activities are designed to be a very pratical and do not depend on artistic or technical abilities.
The way they are designed means experience is important, not the final result.

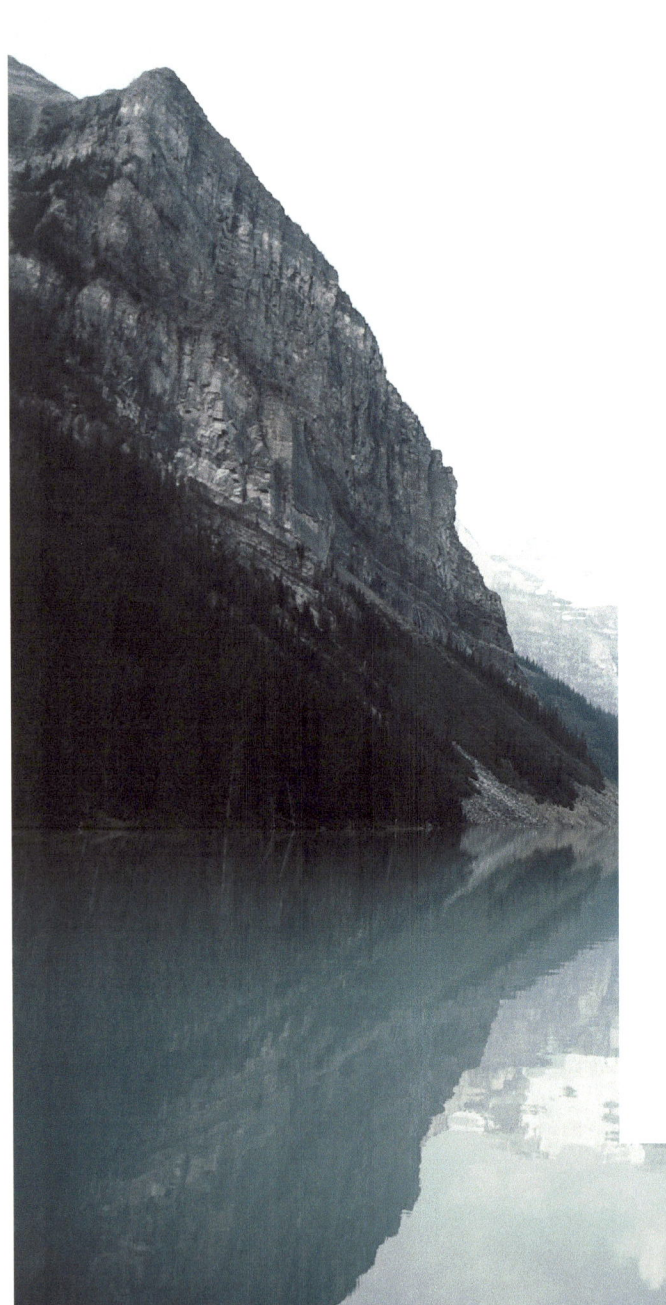

"TREAT EVERYONE YOU MEET AS IF THEY WERE YOU." — DOUG DILLON

The activities are organised for the individual, in small groups as well as through communal group activity. The participant has time to create and work awith one - to collaborate other participants and to work with the group as a whole.

> *"If you are facing in the right direction, all you need to do is keep on walking."*
>
> Buddha

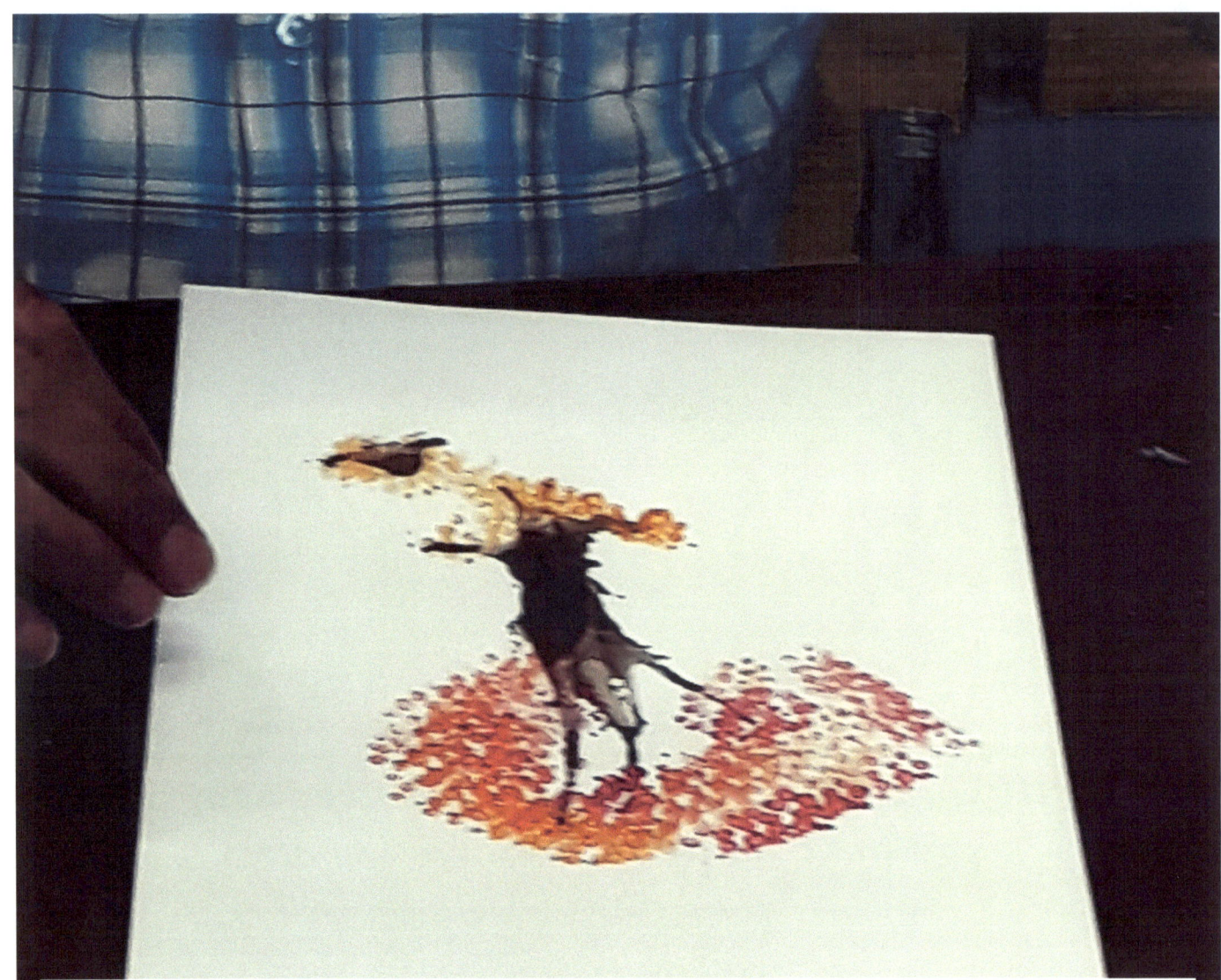

Through guided or spontaneous artistic production, you are able to experience profound benefits

It can be difficult to open up to complete strangers about your deepest darkest emotions. Sometimes we are taught to suppress our emotions and put on a blank face, The simple act of a scribble on paper can likely bring to light darkness, ignite conversation, or be a release for a depressing thought.

ART AS SELF-CARE

HOW ART CAN HELP MONITORING PEOPLE DIAGNOSED WITH BIPOLAR DISORDER,

"Noah Hass-Cohan and Richard Carr hypothesize in Art Therapy and Clinical Neuroscience that the repeated methods of making art and communicating with others through art could have positive effects similar to cognitive behavioral therapy in changing brain functions. With this knowledge individuals may be able to change their behavior leading up to these episodes. They may avoid certain people, activities and places that place them in a negative situation.

The idea that art can help people is based on its expressive nature and its role in emotional and stress release. From a scientific point of view, what happens in the brain when one participates in art may help explain why it is such a therapeutic activity.

Cathy Malchiodi claims, in her book, The Art Therapy Sourcebook, that art connects the mind and body, which can contribute to feelings of mastery and control. Noah Hass-Cohen and Richard Carr indicate that this helps encourage self-expression and reduce the effects of stressors."

NOTHING CAN HARM YOU AS MUCH AS YOUR OWN THOUGHTS UNGUARDED." – BUDDHA

Presentation activity
MARBLE NAIL-POLISH MUG

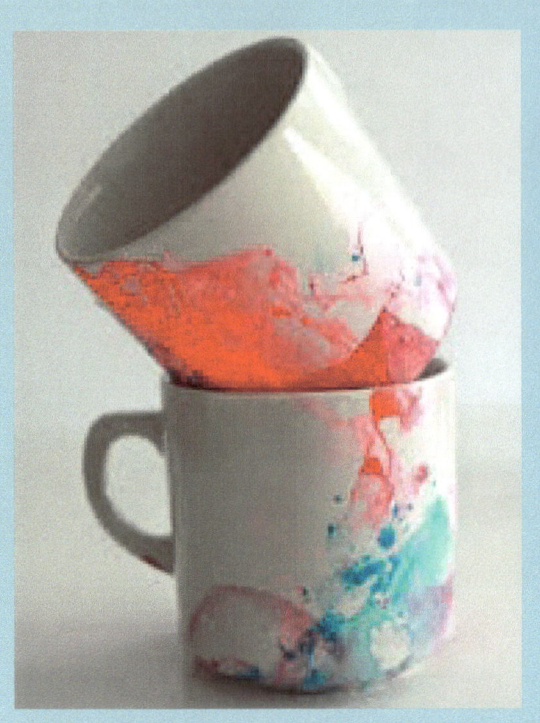

Materials
Coffee mugs (other ceramic or glass items also work)
Nail polish
Toothpicks
Large, disposable plastic container that you don't mind ruining
Paper towel
Nail polish remover (hopefully you won't need it, but just in case)

First, fill your container with hot water. The nail polish dries very fast on the water, so the hotter the better.

Pour your nail polish into the water. Hold the nail polish bottle close to the water, otherwise the drops will fall to the bottom instead of resting on the surface. Instead of making drops, I did swirly lines of nail polish, covering the whole surface of the water with gaps in between the lines. Once the nail polish is on the water, you'll need to work quickly or the polish will dry. Take a toothpick and swirl the nail polish so it covers most of the water. Quickly dip your mug into the polish. Try not to get any on the place where the drinker would put their mouth. Let it sit for a few seconds so the nail polish can cling to the mug. Take your mug out of the water. Turn your mugs upside down on a paper towel to dry.

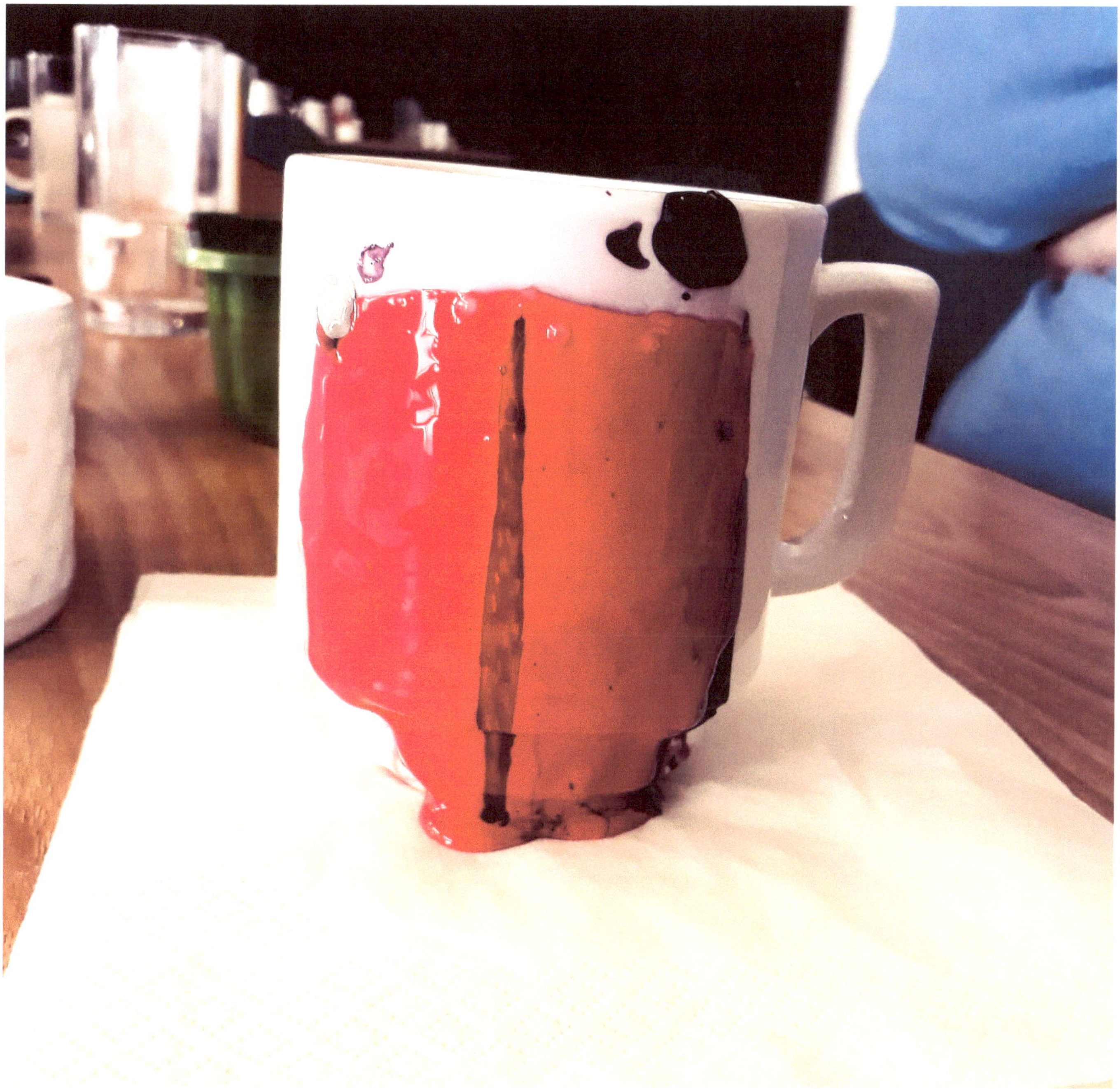

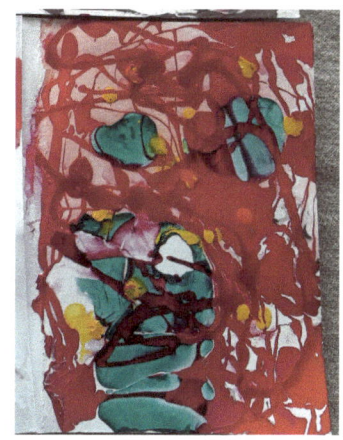
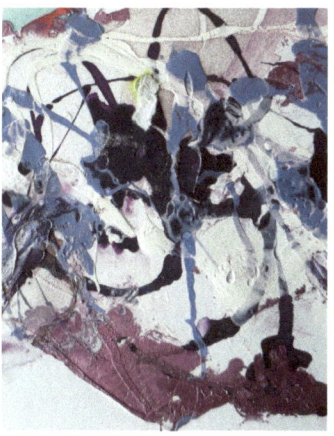
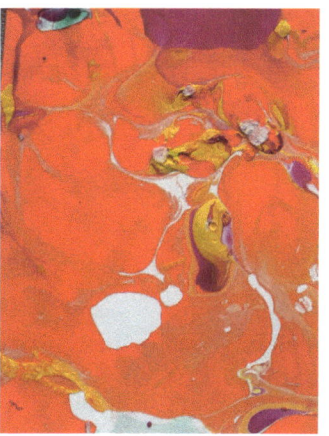
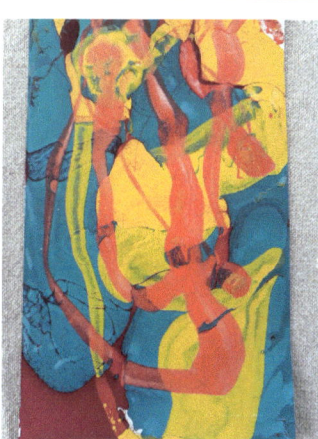

"I TOOK A DEEP BREATH AND LISTENED TO THE OLD BRAG OF MY HEART. I AM, I AM, I AM."
— SYLVIA PLATH, THE BELL JAR

BUSINESS CARD

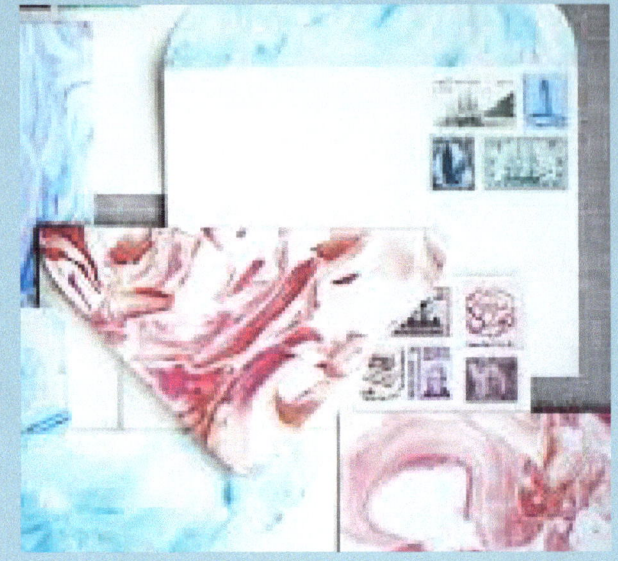

Materials
This is a continuation of the Marble Mug.
Add white paper 300grs
One pen or pencil

Using the same container as for the nail polish, lay a piece of paper in the container, then paint the paper with the polish inside. Let it sit a few seconds so the polish can dry. Lay it on a paper towel to dry.
Whe the paper is dry, scan it, then the instructor will digitally design a personal card for each participant. They can print it.

> "I TOOK A DEEP BREATH AND LISTENED TO THE OLD BRAG OF MY HEART. I AM, I AM, I AM."
> — SYLVIA PLATH, THE BELL JAR

BUSINESS CARD

Materials
This is a continuation of the Marble Mug.
Add white paper 300grs
One pen or pencil

Using the same container as for the nail polish, lay a piece of paper in the container, then paint the paper with the polish inside. Let it sit a few seconds so the polish can dry. Lay it on a paper towel to dry.
Whe the paper is dry, scan it, then the instructor will digitally design a personal card for each participant. They can print it.

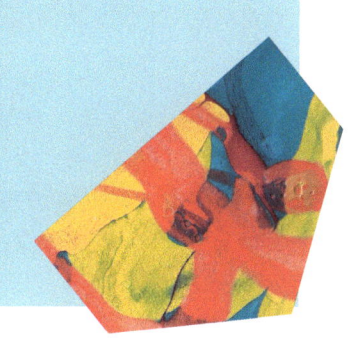

"FEELINGS COME AND GO LIKE CLOUDS IN A WINDY SKY. CONSCIOUS BREATHING IS MY ANCHOR." — THICH NHAT HANH, STEPPING INTO FREEDOM: RULES OF MONASTIC PRACTICE FOR NOVICES

FLOATING LEAVES

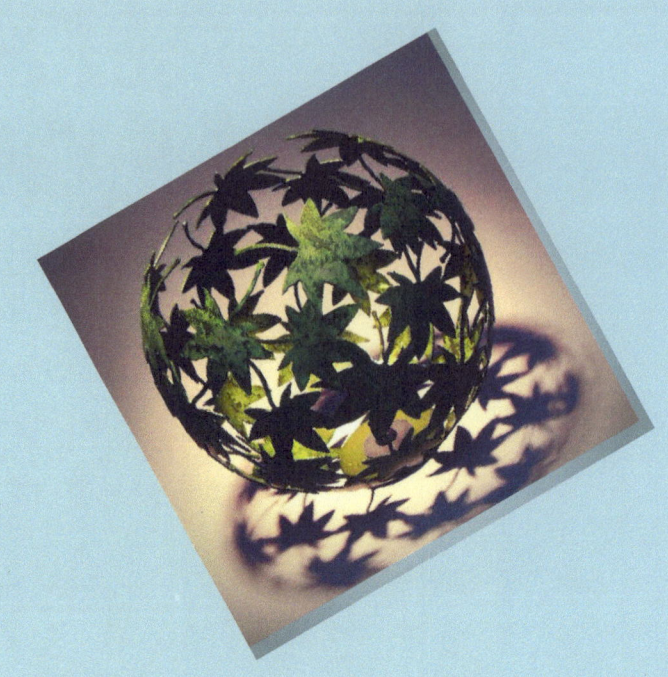

Materials
collect leaves during the walk.
glue
brushes
ballons
string
Blue tack
scissors

Blow up balloon and place in a large bowl for stability. ....Dip the leaves into a glue mixture and add layers of leaves onto the balloon. When the leaves are completely dry, cut a small hole in the bottom nand slowly deflate it. You have created a globe of leaves! We will hang these pieces on the stairwell.

Activity to be performed in pairs or in threes, the participants can make as many ballons as they wish.

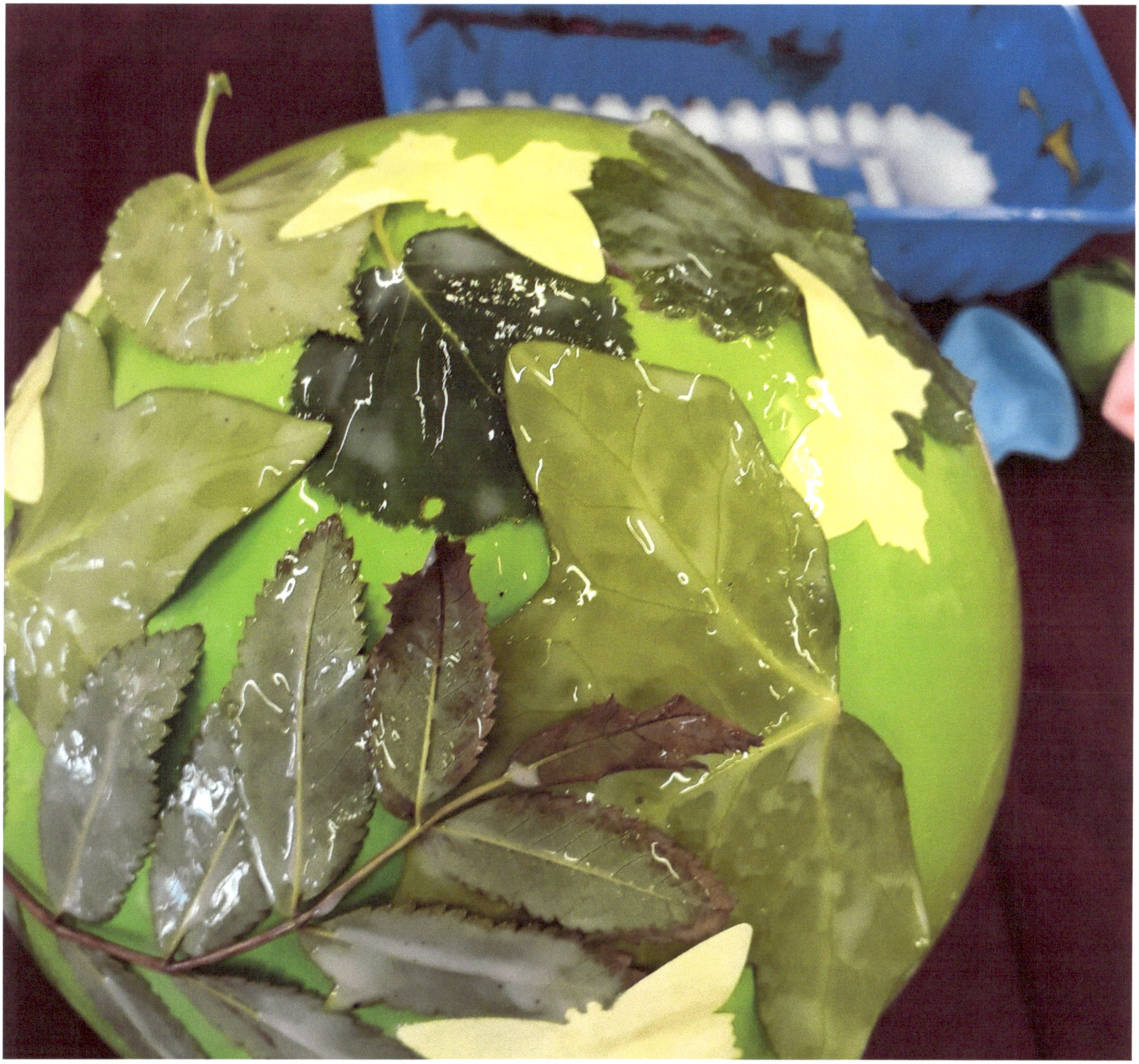

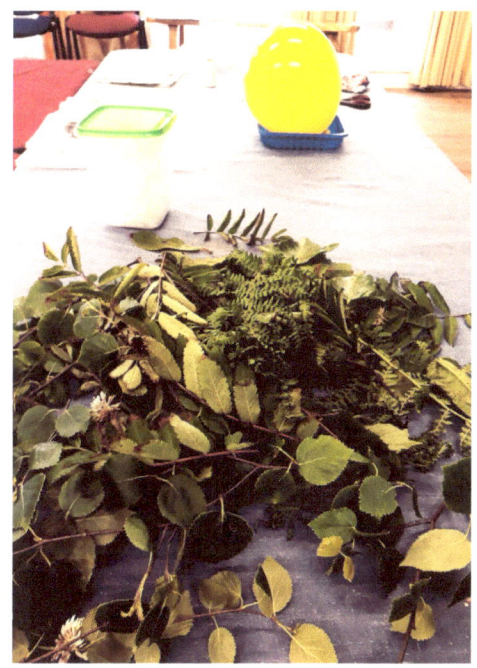
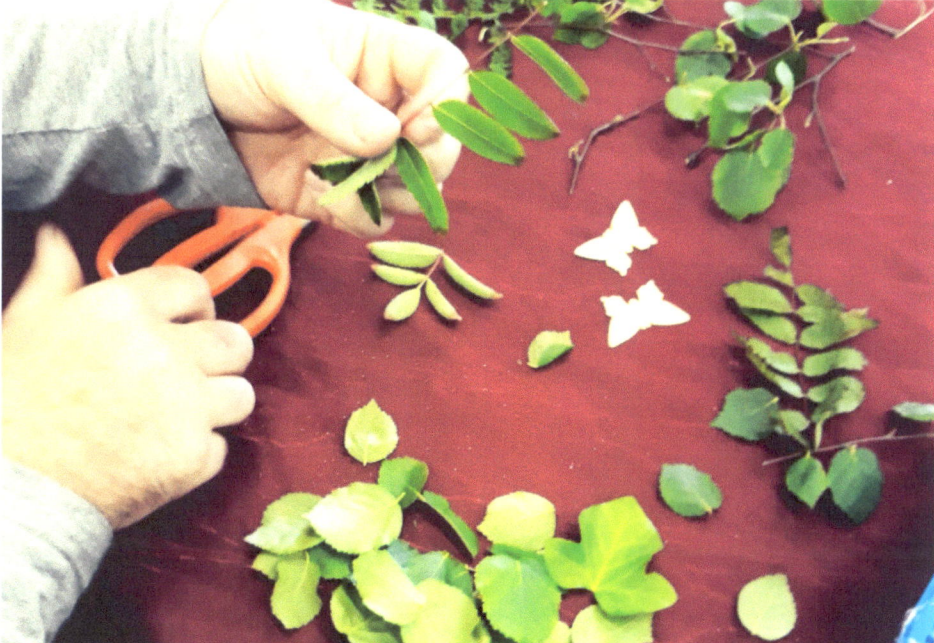

"YOU CANNOT CONTROL THE RESULTS, ONLY YOUR ACTIONS." — ALLAN LOKOS

PAPER ART

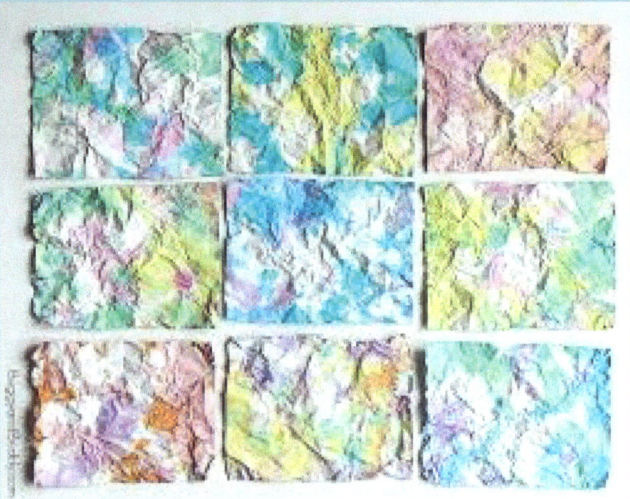

Materials:
White construction paper
Watercolors (liquid watercolors.)
Paintbrush
Scissors or paper cutter

Cut the white construction paper into smaller pieces. We split ours into fourths so we ended up with four 6 inch x 4.5 inch pieces per sheet of construction paper.

Take one piece of your cut construction paper and crumple it up into a ball. dipped in plaster) about 5 minutes after it starts to set, it's still pliable.

Choose one color and use it to paint all around the outside of the ball. Gently unfold it, and see how it looks. Press it down gently. Crumple it up again, and paint it with another color.

Gently unfold it and press it down. Many times we stopped only after two colors, but you can continue this process with a third color if you like.

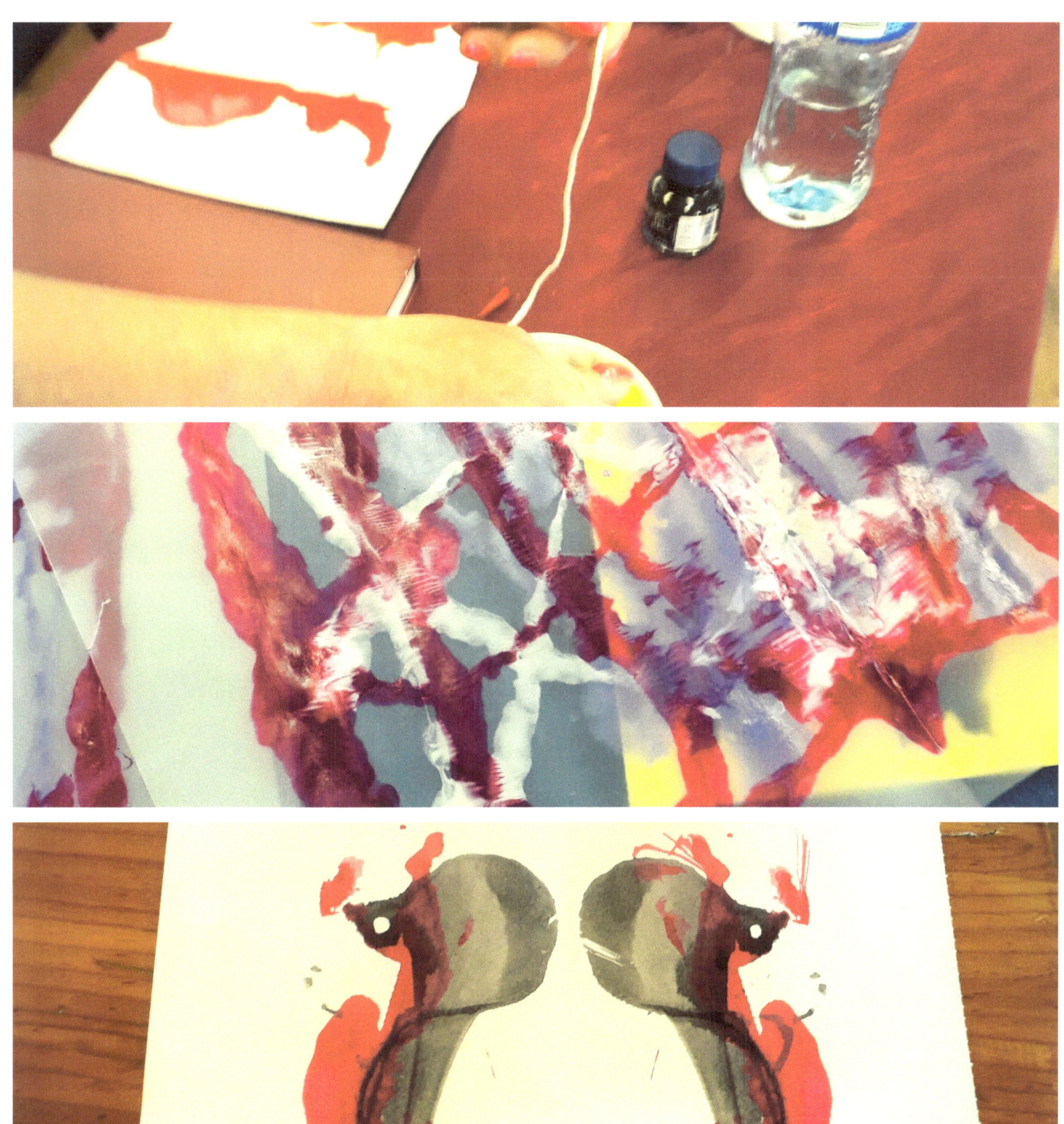

BRANCHES ON A TREE COME FROM THE SAME ROOT, GROW IN DIFFERENT DIRECTIONS, YET ALL COMPLEMENT THE BEAUTY OF THE TREE

BUNDLED Q-TIP TREE

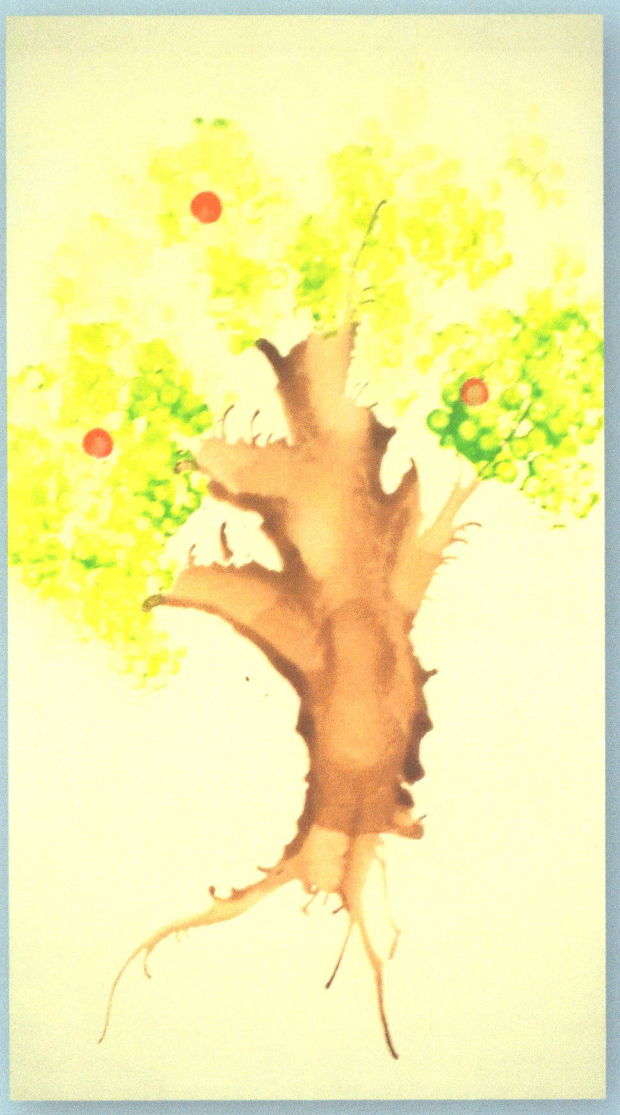

Materials:
Paper
Paint
Q-Tips
Rubber Band
Paint Brush

Paint a paper with a simple bare tree on them. Grab a handful of Q-tips & bundled them together with a rubber band. Squeeze different paints into an old paper bowl. You can dipped the bundled Q-tips into the different colors & pressed the bundle onto our canvas & all around the tree's branches.
Indicividual activity and then done in a group with a single branch.

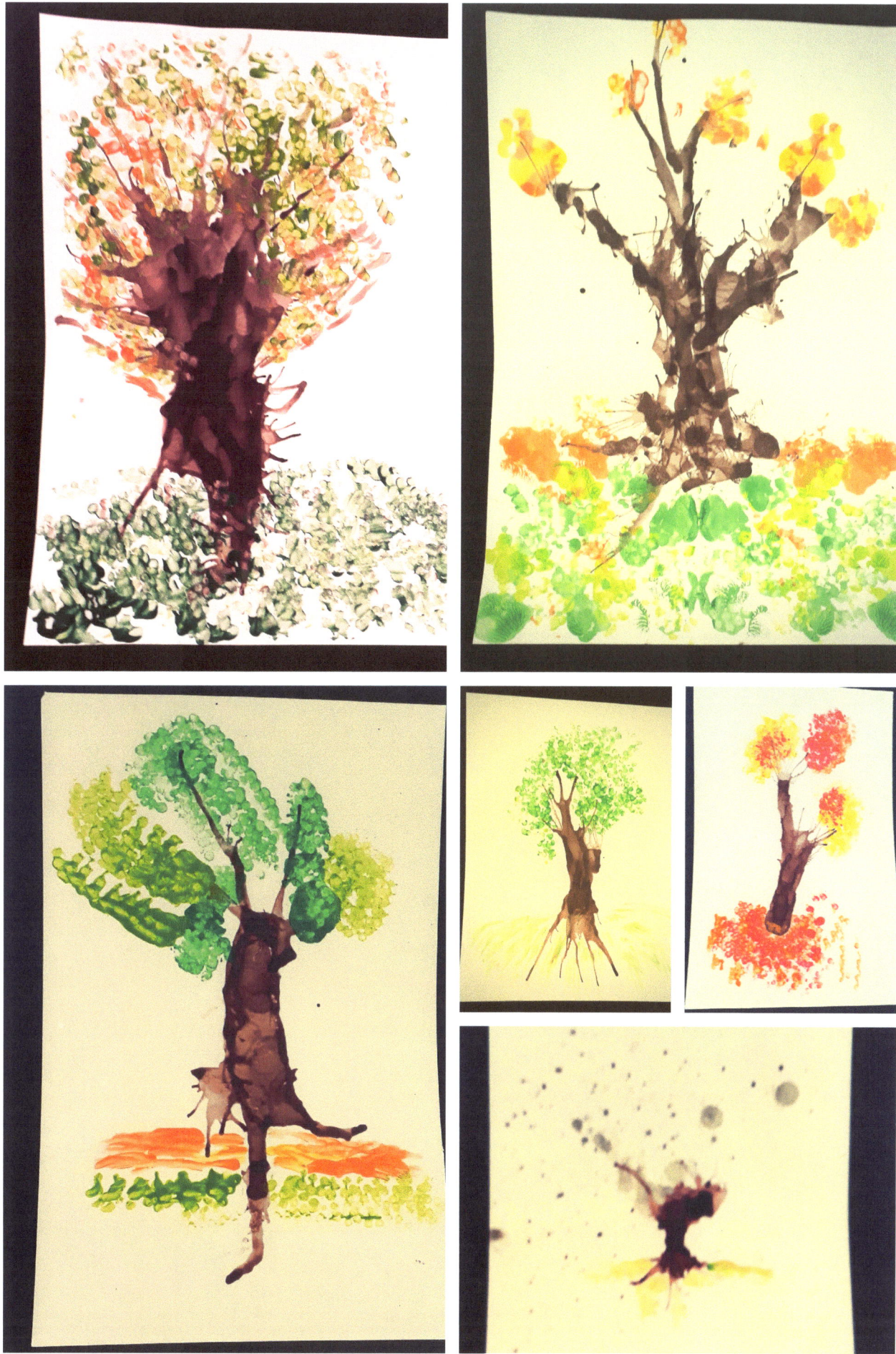

IT'S NOT WHAT YOU LOOK AT THAT MATTERS, IT'S WHAT YOU SEE - HENRY DAVID THOREAU

LIGHT BULB ART

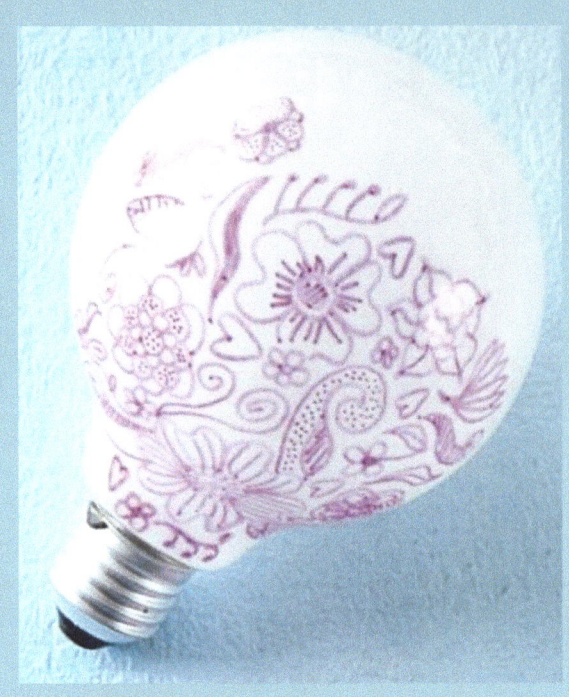

Materials:
bulbs
sharpie pens

Write on a light bulb with a sharpie pen it will cast your designs on the wall.

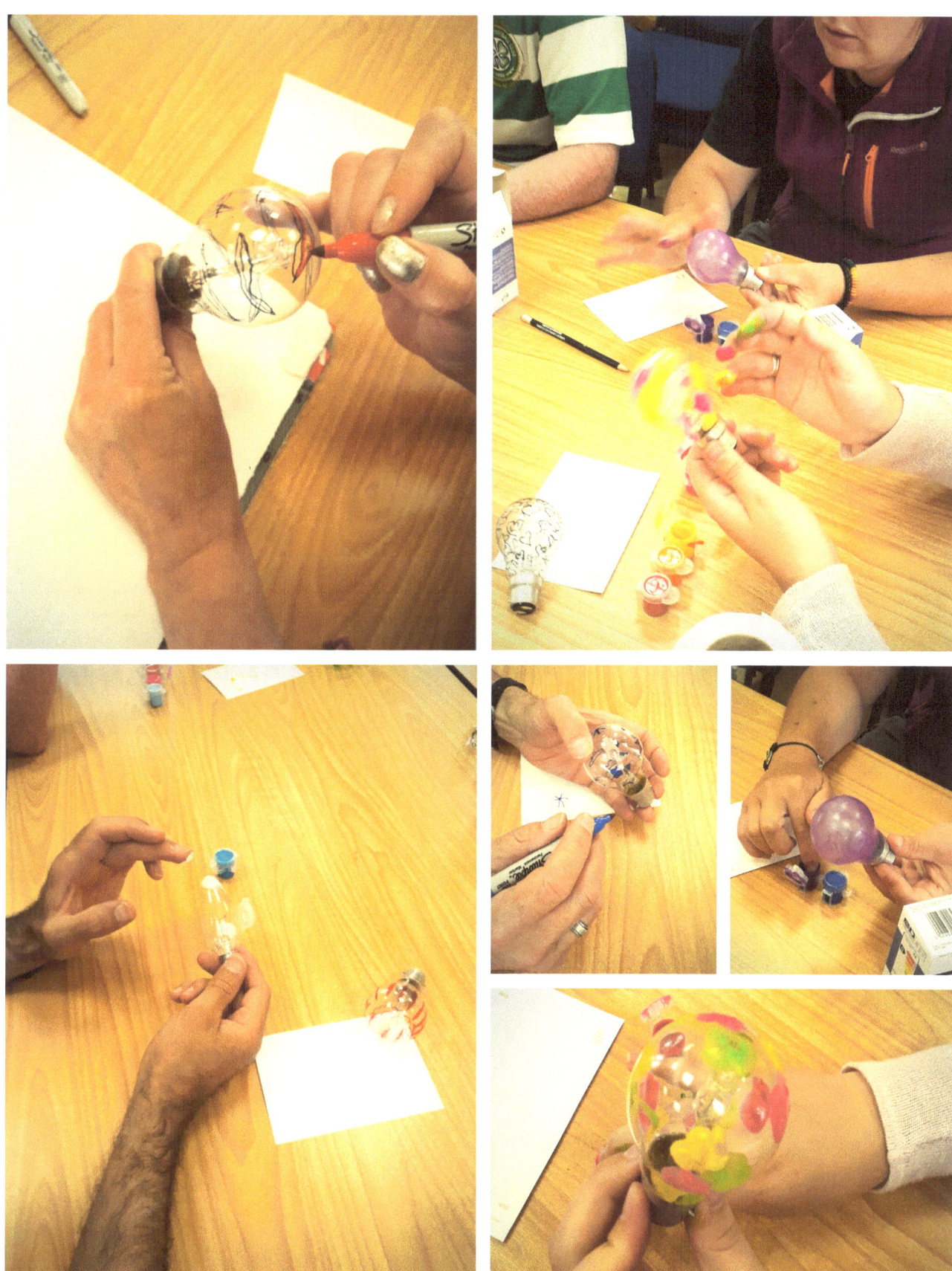

MOVIMENT IS THE SONG OF THE BODY

TINFOIL SCULPTURE

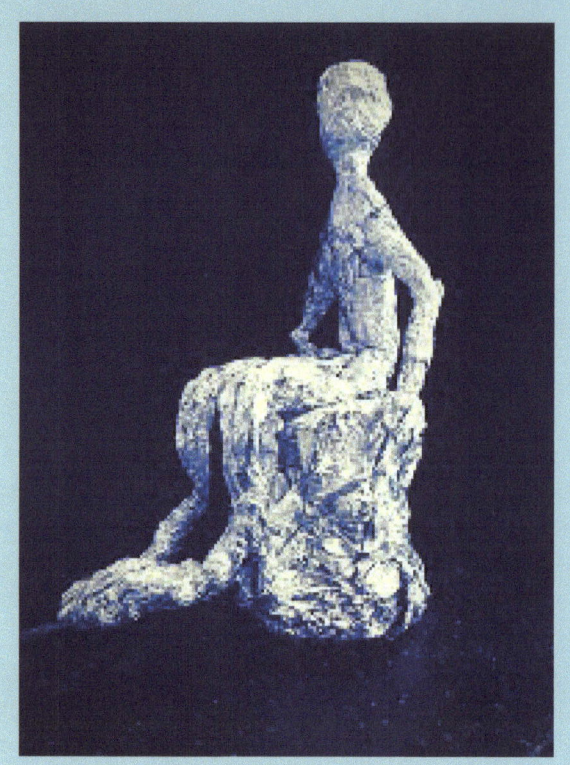

**Materials:
Tinfoil – one roll per person**

Make two cuts 5 inches deep in the top of the tinfoil
Make one cut at the bottom of the tinfoil 5 inches deep
Form a head from the middle piece at the top
Form two arms on either side of the head
Form the legs of tin foil person

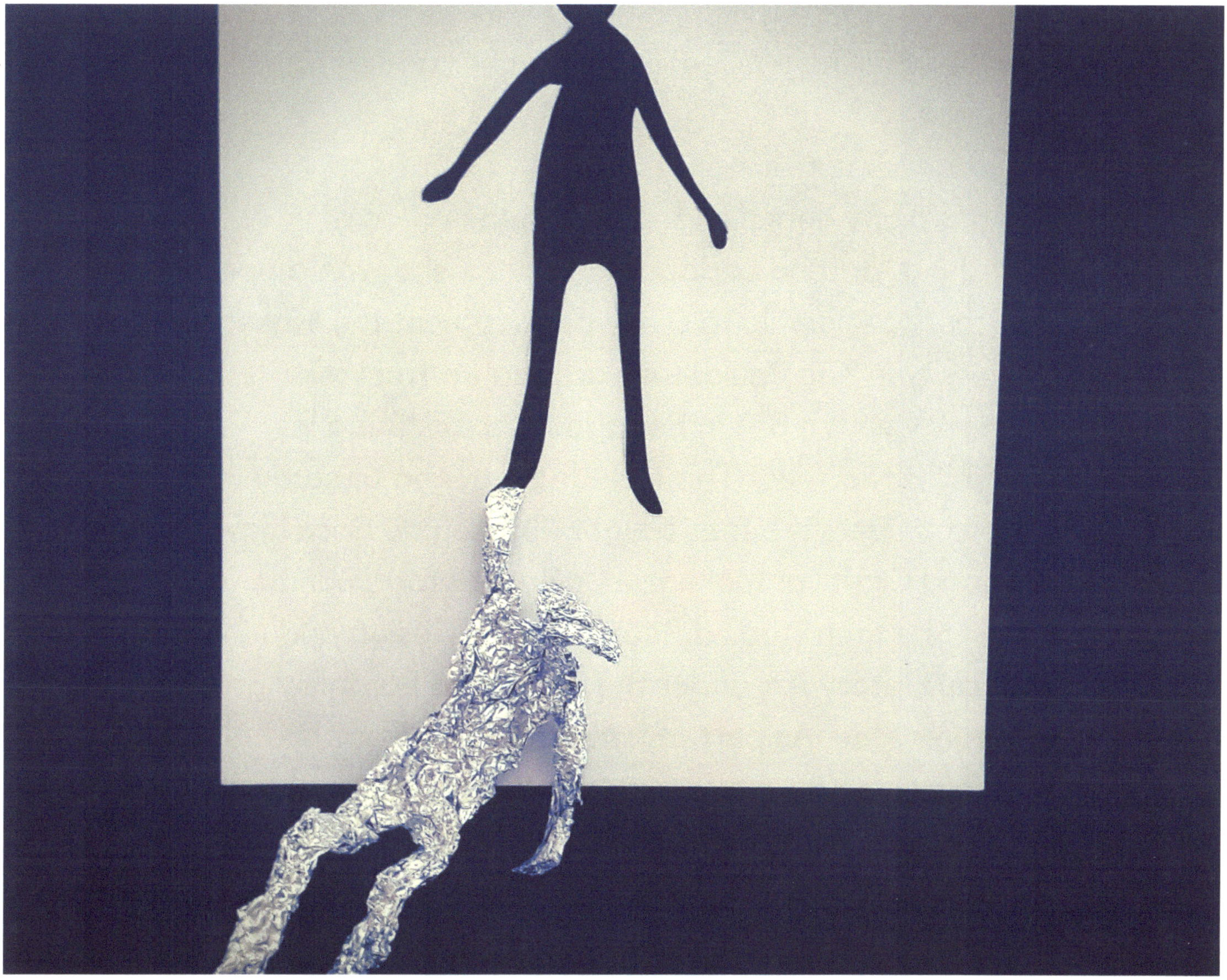

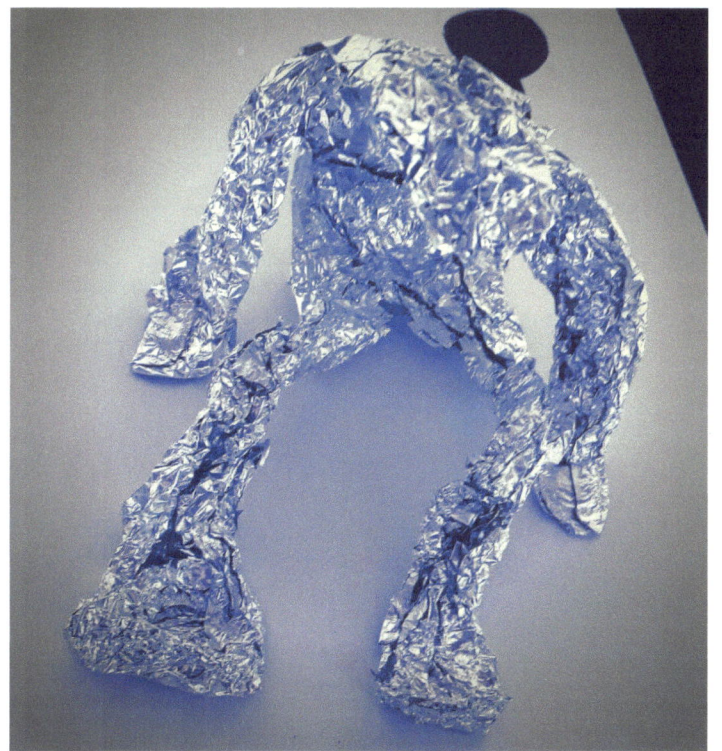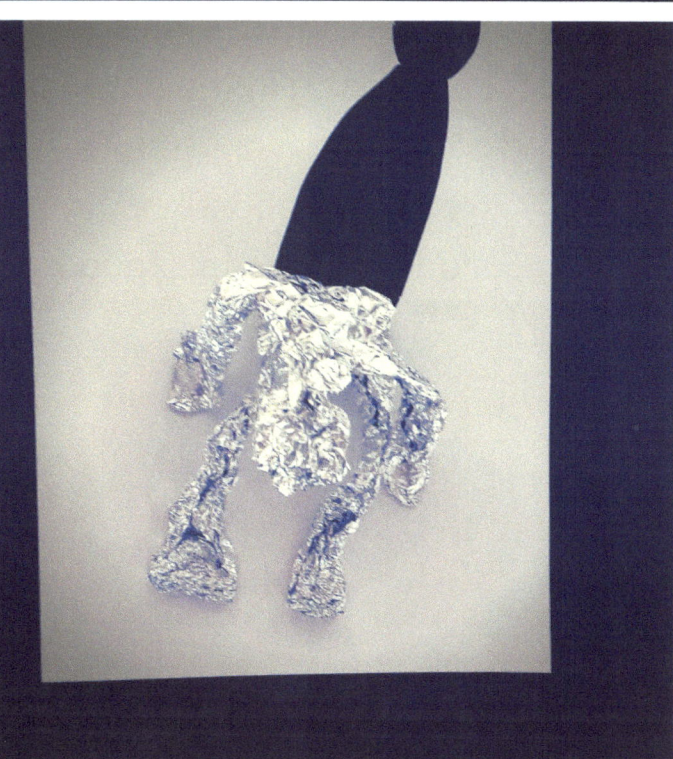

Inês Quintanilha McGee is the teacher and designer of this book.

She has many years' experience in the areas of publishing, art and pedagogy. In 1995, she won a Banco do Brasil scholarship to study pedagogy at the Makensie University in São Paulo. Inês graduated from the University with a B.A in Pedagogy, specialising in learning difficulties. (This included a period of study in Oxford University). Inês taught Philosophy, Sociology, Arts and Crafts at Makenzie University for a number of years. She then studied Botanical Art, Design and Natural History Art under the renowned botanical artist, Margaret Mee. As part of her training, Inês attended tutorials given by the famous Japanese botanical artist, Dra. Hiroi.

Inês worked with ABER (Associação Brasileira de Encadernação e Restauro), a national organisation specialising in the production and repair of handmade books and manuscripts. Inês gained expertise in traditional book-binding and in the creation of hand-made manuscripts/publications.

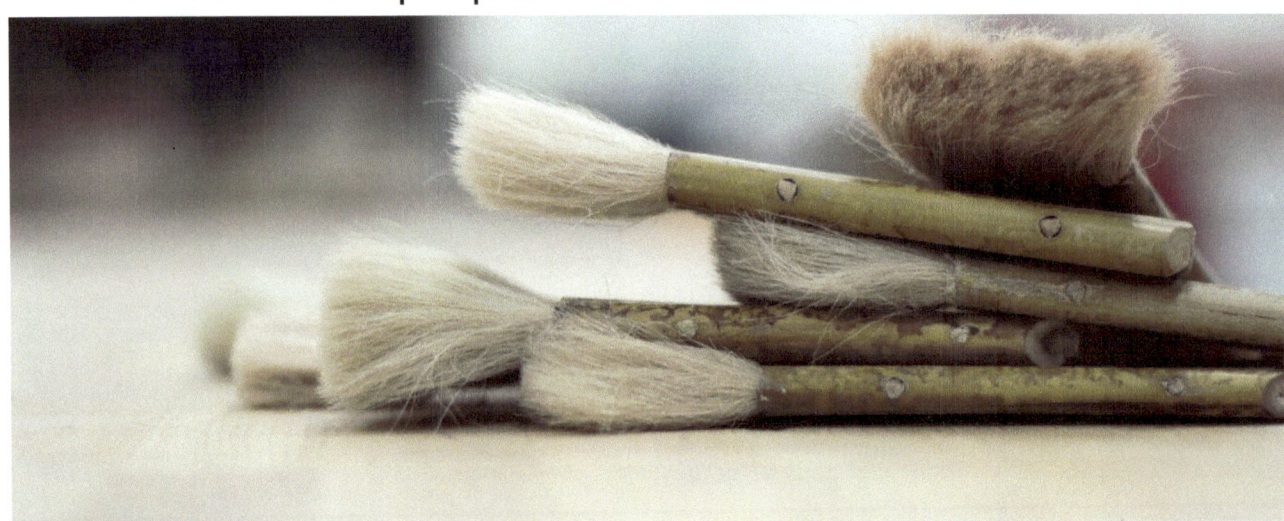

Since 2000, Inês has worked in the publishing business as a publisher, editor, designer and illustrator. She has designed and published over 40 books. Inês has also created teaching materials for schools, particularly for Montessori, Waldorf, schools and Bilingual schools and Mental Health issues institutes.

Great books help you understand, and they help you feel understood.
–John Green

+353 085 804 6836
Form Ireland to the world

www.ingramcontent.com/pod-product-compliance
Lightning Source LLC
Chambersburg PA
CBHW051831210526
45473CB00005B/1827